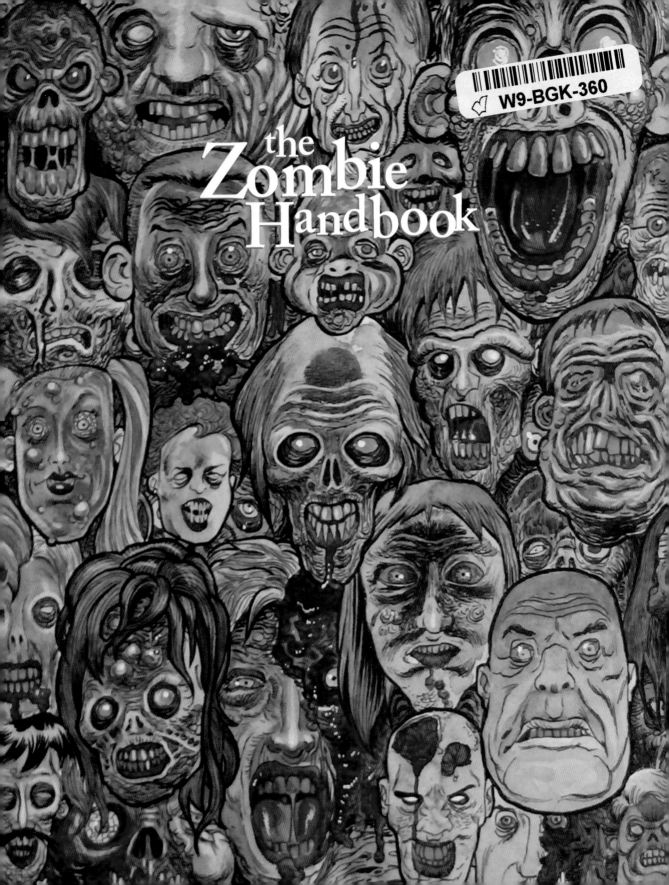

the Zombie Handbook

the Zombie Handbook

How to Identify the Living Dead
and Survive the
Coming Zombie Apocalypse

Rob Sacchetto

Ulysses Press

Published in the United States by
Ulysses Press
P.O. Box 3440
Berkeley, CA 94703
www.ulyssespress.com

ISBN 13: 978-1-56975-705-5

Library of Congress Control Number 2008911765

Printed in Korea by Tara TPS through Four Colour Print Group

10 9 8 7 6 5 4 3 2 1

Contributing writer: Andrea Sacchetto
Acquisitions editor: Nick Denton-Brown
Managing editor: Claire Chun
Editor: Richard Harris
Proofreader: Rebecca Goodberg
Editorial consultant: Clay Martin
Design and layout: what!design @ whatweb.com
Production: Abigail Reser

Distributed by Publishers Group West

Contents

Foreword...6

Introduction to Zombies..............................10

Know Your Zombies.................................... 22

The Zombie Diet...................................... 48

Zombie Life... 60

Surviving the Zombie Apocalypse 74

Our Zombies, Ourselves 98

About the Authors 110

FOREWORD

Zombies.

You can back a vampire down with a cross and some garlic.

You can chase werewolves off with wolfsbane.

You can get a priest to cast out a demon.

None of that works with zombies. Like Terminators, they can't be reasoned with, or bargained with…and they absolutely will not stop until you are dead.

Zombies are the ultimate monster. They inspire paranoia and chew on our insecurities because anyone can become a zombie. Your mother, your best friend, your girlfriend…even your little baby. They present a threat as widespread and constant as the most virulent plague, but unlike the unseen pathogens there is a nightmarish face to this monster. They dig deep into our fear of the unknown because when they rise there often seems to be no clear-cut reason for it. Radiation from a space probe? A toxic spill? A disease that escaped a lab? These are theories, and all of the experts who might have come up with answers have been chomped and chewed. Leaving us alone against the indefatigable hordes of the risen dead.

Nothing else in folklore or fiction is as universally frightening as this cold, mindless, tireless army of the living dead.

The only hope we can cling to is knowledge. The ability to recognize a threat and rationally—despite the dread that gnaws at us—know how to react is the one thing that can allow humanity to survive.

That's why *The Zombie Handbook: How to Identify the Living Dead and Survive the Coming Apocalypse* has become the most crucial manual for survival.

Rob Sacchetto has always been a leader among erosion artists—that special kind of artist who can look into the face of the undead and see the human that was and the monster that is. His "Know Your Zombies" poster is widely regarded as a landmark public safety announcement, and it's certainly saved lives from Canada to Mexico.

It saved mine, I can tell you that.

Rob has an eye for zombies. He can spot 'em, and he knows how to capture their essence on canvas so that everyone who sees his work will be on the alert. His *Zombie Handbook* is a must-have for anyone who wants to make it home alive.

You're reading this now, so you have a copy. The images and common-sense advice packed into this book are at your fingertips.

If you are reading this…then you're alive.

Keep this book handy. As long as zombies walk the earth, you're going to need Rob Sacchetto close at hand to keep you safe.

Jonathan Maberry

Multiple Bram Stoker Award–winning author of *Patient Zero* (St. Martins Griffin) and *Zombie CSU: The Forensics of the Living Dead* (Citadel Press). www.jonathanmaberry.com

Introduction to Zombies

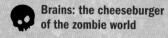
Brains: the cheeseburger of the zombie world

What Are Zombies?

Zombies have existed for the whole of human history. They are only recently coming to public attention, however, because of the startling rise in infection rates around the globe.

The term "zombie" generally describes any dead creature that has come back to life or has been suspended in "living death." Zombies may be under the control of outside, usually evil, forces—such as aliens, madmen, cults or military scientists. Over the last few decades, however, the term has come to refer more specifically to the dead who return to feast on the living, especially their brains.

Studies Show

The average zombie consumes up to eight pounds of brains a day.

The average zombie lifespan is 2.34 years. Although in theory they can live indefinitely, their bodies fall apart (literally) over time until they can no longer seek out the flesh that sustains them.

Judging from the extent of decomposition, this zombie is estimated to be six-and-a-half years old—ancient by zombie standards.

Vacant stare

Foreign objects embedded in body

Drool

Rotting flesh

Oozing pus or blood

Missing body parts

Shredded clothing

Stiffness in body and limbs

Visible bone protruding from flesh

Zombie Characteristics

Zombies are a heterogeneous bunch, as diverse within their species as we humans are within ours. Yet most zombies share certain distinguishing characteristics.

The Zombie Shuffle

Many zombies walk with a shuffling gait in which they drag one leg behind the other. This slow limp typically results from wounds suffered before zombification or from uneven decomposition afterward. But not all zombies are so handicapped. Many are able-bodied enough to achieve impressive land speeds.

Where Do Zombies Come From?

No one knows how the first zombie originated, though sightings have been recorded since the time of ancient man. All we know is how zombies spread: typically, from other zombies transmitting the virus via infectious attack.

Many zombies, however, are created through corpse reanimation. Corpses susceptible to reanimation can be found in graveyards, morgues, evil laboratories, mortuaries, old decrepit mausoleums, war zones, pet cemeteries, nursing homes, shopping malls, churches, or medical schools that use cadavers.

 Cemeteries: final resting place of the deceased—or zombie petri dish?

The Zombie Virus

Current theory suggests that zombies are brought back to life by a virus. The zombie virus is frustratingly elusive to researchers, as it mutates rapidly and can vary greatly from one epidemic to the next. Some general characteristics of the virus, however, are universal. First, it is highly contagious. Any contact involving even the slightest fluid exchange will turn you into a zombie. How quickly and violently this takes place depends on the strain of the virus and the individual's immune system.

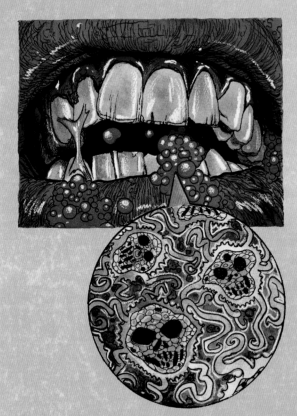

 The zombie virus on a microscopic slide, enlarged four million times. Note the flesh- and soul-eating viroids.

Transmission of the Zombie Virus

Though biting is the most common means by which zombieism is passed on, the virus may also be contracted through zombie scratches or abrasions.

Likewise, an airborne virus may also turn a human into a zombie without any biting. With the airborne strain, death itself is the catalyst that triggers the virus. Although scientists are unsure as to exactly how the airborne virus is contracted, once it establishes itself within a host, it is completely undetectable and only reveals itself at the time of death, when it causes reanimation.

Biting is not the only form of zombie transmission. Zombie-inflicted scratches will transform this unfortunate woman into one of the undead.

Scientists are working to find a way to protect humans from the zombie virus.

Stage 1: Immediately after zombie bite

Stage 2: One hour later

Stage 3: After complete zombification

Effects of Zombie Attacks on Live Humans

Zombies typically inflict wounds on humans through biting, hitting, scratching or other direct physical assaults, as they lack the manual dexterity to handle weapons. Some exceptionally strong and violent zombies have even been known to slap faces, or sometimes entire heads, off their victims.

Whether a human is infected from a zombie bite or scratch, an airborne virus, fluid exchange, or an all-out zombie feeding frenzy, the outcome remains the same: the victim is always zombified.

Whether zombies attack individually or in a horde is purely coincidental. They have no instinct for strategy. As the attackee, it is clearly better to be attacked individually. If you are attacked by a swarm of zombies, you have little hope for escape.

A zombie horde attacks a single human.

Human remains after all-out zombie horde attack

Zombies: Before and After

Compare the same human male before and after zombification. Notice the subtle differences. The skin changes from a pinkish tone to blackish green. The eyes hollow and take on an unhealthy yellowish hue. Before zombification, there are no visible bones. After, the skin is torn away in several places. Blood pools at the zombie's feet, which is not normal in an unzombified human. If you see someone exhibiting these symptoms, it is probably a zombie.

There are several ways to tell if someone you love is turning into a zombie. Tragically, you have to act fast if you want to save yourself. The longer you wait to dispatch an infected loved one—a nine-iron to the back of the head is especially effective—the higher the risk. Here are a few signs to look for if someone has been infected and is transforming into a zombie.

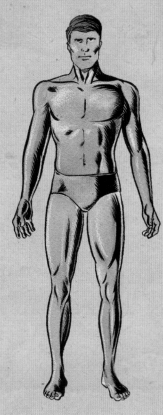
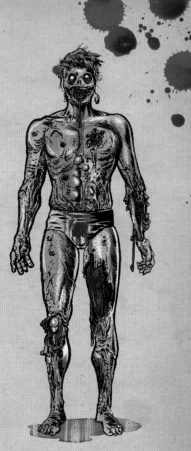

Before   **After**

Zombification Checklist

- Low moaning and groaning from victim
- Festering boils and oozing wounds on the skin
- Blank, staring or milky eyes
- Body convulsions that stop abruptly
- Black gums and blue lips
- Recessed eyes

- Odor of bad ham
- Lack of bladder or bowel control
- Clammy, cold or slimy skin
- Vomiting up internal organs
- Blue veins visible through pale skin
- Clamoring for brains

Zombies of the World

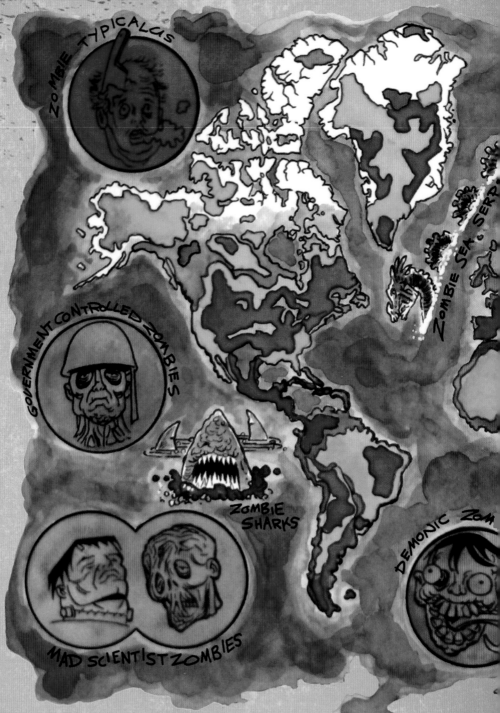

ZOMBIE TYPICALUS

GOVERNMENT CONTROLLED ZOMBIES

ZOMBIE SHARKS

MAD SCIENTIST ZOMBIES

ZOMBIE SEA SERP...

DEMONIC ZOM...

ALIEN CONTROLLED ZOMBIES

APATHY ZOMBIES

VOODOO ZOMBIES

ZOMBIE PIRATE WATERS

Even in the time of Gilgamesh, zombies posed a threat.

Zombies in History and Legend

Zombies are as ancient as human history itself. The first recorded instance of zombieism dates back to the ancient tale of Gilgamesh (c. 2700 BCE), in which Princess Ishtar threatened her father, King Anu, saying that she would "let the dead to go up and eat the living." Fortunately, that zombie outbreak was averted, and humankind was spared.

Like today's living dead, the first zombies exemplified the risk involved in tampering with the unknown. Take the golem, for example. Not entirely typical of zombies, this creature of lifeless clay in human form could be brought to life in a time of need. One of the first golems was brought to life by a rabbi in defense of Jews in a Prague ghetto around the year 1600. But the golem grew to enormous size, became unruly and turned on its master, prompting the rabbi to exclaim, "Oy, gevalt, what have I done?!"

The moral of the story of the golem: Once unleashed, zombies are impossible to contain.

In 14th-century Lithuania, alchemist Stiena Corblast fell in love with a villager who lived at the foot of the mountain beneath his castle. The young woman was happily married to a handsome blacksmith, but this did not deter Corblast, who began creating a homunculus to do his bidding. Once finished, the alchemist transferred his life into the creature with complex incantations. Corblast planned to have his monster do away with the husband and bring the widow back to his castle. But while his body lay in a suspended state, spilled chemicals ignited a fire that engulfed the castle, killing Corblast and trapping his soul in the homunculus. Meanwhile, the creature peered into the village couple's window and saw how happy they were. The realization that his soul was trapped in a horrifying monster washed over him. Corblast stayed his hand and ran weeping into the forest. Though the fate of the homunculus is unclear, it may account for sightings that still occur to this day of a Bigfoot-like creature in the forests of Eastern Europe.

Pictured here is one of the few human-sized homunculi.

A patchwork humanoid—a composite made from parts of several dead bodies—is usually the work of a madman with a Ph.D., a God complex and a laboratory in an old, abandoned castle. The first known patchwork humanoid, Frankenstein's monster, appeared in 1818. Despite its obvious similarities to the typical zombie, this creature retained much of its humanity.

The original zombie poster child

A Haitian necromancer commanding his living "zombie"

At the same time, half a world away, zombies were being created by the voodoo practitioners of Haiti, where the actual word "zombie" originated. Haitian zombies are victims of a neurotoxin delivered through bodily wounds by voodoo priests called hougans or mambos. The toxic potion brings about a deathlike state. Virtually undetectable even by physicians, the poison works its sinister magic, whereupon the victim is pronounced dead, buried and, after a few days, exhumed by the voodoo priest, who then enslaves the victim and uses him as cheap labor or as an instrument of revenge. If the Haitian zombie ingests meat or salt, it will break the voodoo spell. If only true zombies could be killed so easily.

Know your Zombies

Know Your Enemies

In the fight against zombies, it is of utmost importance to understand your enemy. Only by truly understanding the nature of the beast can you become the best zombie killer that you can be. Not learning how zombies think and act could be the last mistake you'll ever make.

In this chapter, you will learn all about the "common zombie" (Zombie Typicalis) as well as other, rarer zombie species. You will learn to identify their individual traits and specific features and come to understand how to deal with them effectively. You never know when you'll come face-to-face with a zombie, and when that moment comes, you'll need to know both what type of living dead you are up against and how to kill it. Be ever vigilant.

☠ Is this a Recently Dead Zombie or a Demonic Possession Zombie? Not knowing the answer could cost you your life.

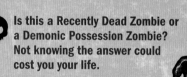

Understanding Zombies

Zombies vary greatly from one to another. Yes, they all devour brains, but not all of them use the same methods. They have different strengths and weaknesses, each of which can be turned to your advantage. For example, zombies with an excellent brain-smelling sense can easily be duped into a trap with a brain lure. Those who are exceptionally strong but slow can only be beaten by engaging in long-range battle.

Every Zombie Is Unique

Like snowflakes, no two zombies are alike. Each possesses the attributes of its particular species. Beyond that, zombies are individuals, each with its own particular tastes and disposition. Failing to understand this has been the downfall of many a zombie hunter.

The Recently Dead Zombie (RDZ)

The two distinct forms of the "common zombie" are the Recently Dead Zombie and the Exhumed Corpse Zombie. The Recently Dead Zombie looks remarkably like the average human, but may show signs of slight to gross physical trauma and can appear confused and disheveled. It may be difficult to spot RDZs until they are up close because their movements remain so fluid and humanlike. Their flesh is mostly intact, with little decay. This species of zombie is highly mobile and should be avoided at all costs. When in RDZ territory, always be prepared to act quickly. If confrontation proves necessary, you can neutralize an RDZ by inflicting a massive head wound.

Distinguishing Features

- Obvious physical trauma
- Copious salivation
- Mostly intact clothing
- Non-advanced decomposition
- Loss of bladder/bowel control
- Temporary stiffening of joints due to rigor mortis

Recently Dead Zombie Traits

Where found: Everywhere

Anatomy: Humanoid

Strengths: Impervious to pain; extremely patient; highly developed sense of smell

Weaknesses: Overwhelming hunger may cloud judgment

Temperament: Highly irritable and violent

Favorite attack method: Violent grappling

Best killed by: Severe head trauma, incineration, vaporization or high voltage

RDZ Awareness

From afar, Recently Dead Zombies look similar to you and me. Most still wear whatever they died in and do not show acute signs of decay. Suspect everyone. Trust no one.

RDZs are most easily identified by signs of trauma and relatively un-decomposed skin. Gaping, bloody wounds or embedded weapons, along with pale, not-yet-green skin, are reliable indicators of a Recently Dead Zombie.

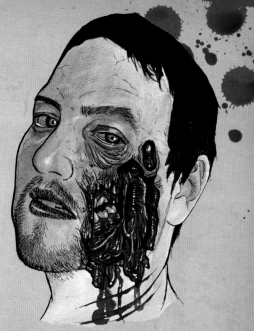

Note the relatively healthy skin and gross physical trauma to the cheek, clear indicators of a Recently Dead Zombie.

Can You Spot the Zombie?
Which of these are Recently Dead Zombies?

Answers appear below.

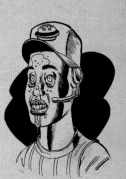

Answers: The doctor, football player and police officer are all RDZs. The fast-food worker is a typical American teenager.

Rob Sacchetto

The Exhumed Corpse Zombie (ECZ)

Included within the Zombie Typicalis species are Exhumed Corpse Zombies, perhaps the foulest of the walking dead. These corpses have spent years, or even centuries, ripening underground before clawing their way back to the surface to feed. Depending on their specific state of decomposition, ECZs may take vastly differing forms. Some may be thin, dry and skeletal, while others may be bloated and dripping with pus.

Most Exhumed Corpse Zombies move rather slowly, as their connective tissue, joints and muscles have deteriorated. They are found in larger groups, usually following their faster Recently Dead counterparts to sources of human flesh. Although these rotting, maggot-ridden zombies may seem harmless and even comical because of their deliberate pace, you should exercise extreme caution. Their great numbers and mob mentality can easily overwhelm overconfident prey.

Distinguishing Features
- Advanced decomposition
- Skeletal in build
- Dressed well in burial/period clothes
- Dry, cracked skin
- Dry, unmanageable hair
- Extremities eaten off by grave beetles

Exhumed Corpse Zombie Traits
Where found: Graveyards

Anatomy: Humanoid (often missing limbs)

Strengths: In numbers

Weaknesses: Slow-moving; clumsy

Temperament: Ill-tempered when first exhumed, then lethargic

Favorite attack method: Horde attack

Best killed by: Head trauma, acid

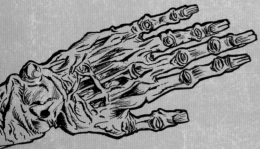

A field sketch of an Exhumed Corpse Zombie's hand. Dehydration and decomposition pulls the skin back from the nail, causing it to appear longer.

Identifying Exhumed Corpse Zombies

Some ECZs have been rotting underground for so long that almost no epidermis remains on their frame. Once risen from their graves, ECZs can appear as little more than walking tendons, shriveled muscle and calcified bone.

An Exhumed Corpse Zombie after three years in the ground. Note the lack of recognizable skin and almost complete absence of hair.

Skin Sloughing

As the fat beneath its flesh begins to liquefy, an ECZ may shed its skin all at once and wander around skinless. Graveyards may become littered with this "footie-pajama-like" flesh as Exhumed Corpse Zombies' skin liquefies and is shed.

Massive Gas Attack

Due to the combustible gases that build up in a corpse, ECZs have been known to vomit large amounts of maggots and insects onto their victims. Sometimes the gas buildup is so great that the ECZ spontaneously explodes. Do not inhale or ingest any of the infectious gore that spews out. Because of their toxicity, ECZs pose a greater threat to humans than previously thought.

World's Fattest Zombie

Buried in a piano crate in 1975, Patrick Doody went into the ground at 875 pounds and emerged as a whopping 925-pound Exhumed Corpse Zombie, bloated with several thousand worms, maggots and grave beetles. Needless to say, he used the smother attack method on his victims.

The Demonic Zombie

Aptly known as the "evil dead," Demonic Zombies can be of the living or dead flesh variety and are controlled by forces of Hell that are intent on stealing souls. These horrible creatures are born out of demonic possession and can be extremely difficult to kill by any method other than advanced exorcism. Demonic Zombies are similar in many respects to other zombies, but tend to be even more ferocious, because they are literally Hell's minions. They are known to twist the flesh of their victims into hideous monstrosities.

Unlike regular zombies, Demonic ones won't stop at just eating flesh. They want your eternal soul and will do anything to get it. They often employ trickery and may even go so far as to shapeshift into the likeness of a loved one to lull a victim into a false sense of security. They may also take possession of inanimate objects in an attempt to drive their victims mad.

Distinguishing Features

- Soulless red or yellow eyes
- Extra-long tongue
- Claws
- Soul pustules
- Extremely distorted facial features

Demonic Zombie Traits

Where found: Old remote cabins

Anatomy: Humanoid (but may possess inanimate objects)

Strengths: Impervious to trauma; must be killed by magic

Weaknesses: Easily destroyed by spells and incantations

Temperament: Highly irritable

Favorite attack method: Soul-sucking

Best killed by: Precision exorcism

Soul Suckers
and Body Possessors

Their ability to suck souls from humans makes Demonic Zombies unique among the living dead. The stolen souls remain with the Demonic Zombie in pustule-like sacs on its skin until it returns to Hell. If the zombie is vanquished, the souls return to their rightful owners or final resting places.

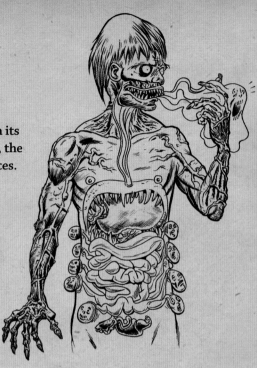

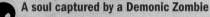

A soul captured by a Demonic Zombie

An inside look at how a Demonic Zombie alters its host's digestive system to accommodate its soul containment system

Tears provide the natural lubricant needed for swallowing souls. The Demonic Zombie grows a long, abrasive tongue that can completely empty the human head of this vital fluid.

Demonic Possession

Demonic Zombies have been known to possess parts of the body, either attached or severed. They can reanimate a hand for wielding a weapon, a head for insulting or an eyeball for spying.

The Mad Scientist Zombie (Type A)

Some zombielike monsters are built by disturbed individuals with Ph.D.s in Biomechanical Science. These walking nightmares have been given life in attempts to create a new breed of human or to prolong one's own existence. They come in two types. One is the human collage, made from parts of cadavers. These may display stitches where differing limbs and extremities have been attached. Created in secret labs or old, remote castles, these creatures exhibit at least some level of intellect and humanlike behavior. But do not allow this to cloud your judgment in dealing with them. Dispatching these composite humanoids calls for extreme measures. Fire is an effective weapon for both keeping them at bay and utterly destroying them. They are not contagious, but may attempt to bite and scratch like animals if cornered.

Mad Scientist Zombie Type A Facts

It took over 347 feet of stitches to assemble the first Mad Scientist Zombie. The original monster was made with select body parts from a variety of cadavers, hence its incredible strength.

The amount of electricity needed to give life to a MSZ is enough to light the Las Vegas Strip for two whole nights—a huge amount of raw energy.

Distinguishing Features

- Neck bolts
- Pale skin
- Stitches where limbs have been affixed
- Mismatched body parts
- Abnormally square head
- Tall, lurching stature

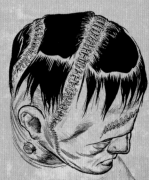

Mad Scientist Zombie Type A Traits

Where found: The countryside, old castles

Anatomy: Composite humanoid

Strengths: Abnormally strong; pain-resistant; can tolerate extreme weather

Weaknesses: Fire, broken heart

Temperament: Enraged

Favorite attack method: Pummeling

Best killed by: Angry mob with torches

The Mad Scientist Zombie (Type B)

The other kind of MSZ is highly contagious and originates on small, usually uncharted islands where a madman can work anonymously and have access to island natives as test subjects. These zombies have been known to turn on the scientist and try to reach the mainland in search of human prey by concealing themselves on passing boats or simply walking across the ocean floor. A note of caution: When traveling by boat in the South Seas, always check your vessel thoroughly for rotting stowaways before departure.

Distinguishing Features:
- Resemblance to island natives
- Poorly stitched
- Dressed in loincloths or less
- Dirty fingernails
- Large surgical scars
- Lazy, disoriented demeanor

Mad Scientist Zombie Type B Traits

Where found: Remote South Seas or Mediterranean islands

Anatomy: Humanoid

Strengths: In numbers

Weaknesses: Island rhythms

Temperament: Perpetually confused, angry, and hungry

Favorite attack method: Frenzied mauling

Best killed by: Fire

Underwater Zombies

"B" type MSZs can survive underwater, often traveling along the sea floor from their remote islands to areas with more plentiful prey. MSZs may sustain themselves on their sea journey with the flesh of sea creatures such as great white sharks.

Government Experiment Zombie

It should come as no surprise that the government has kept the public in the dark about its involvement in secret zombie research and development. Government Experiment Zombies are the result of the military's decades-long search to perfect the ultimate soldier. They were first created through electrochemical science and then perfected using a sprayable toxin administered to corpses. The first of these zombified soldiers were quite docile and agreeable, but as with most attempts to exploit the living dead, they soon turned on their superiors. The ensuing catastrophe halted further study, and the zombies were stored safely away from the public...or so everyone thought. From time to time they have resurfaced, forcing the military to take swift, decisive action and then cover up horrible atrocities. Because of their military training and background, these zombies pose a serious threat to their victims.

Distinguishing Features
- Camouflage fatigues
- Clean-cut
- Expressionless
- Grey, pale skin
- Physically fit (for a dead guy)
- Army helmet

Government Experiment Zombie Traits

Where found: Secret army bases

Anatomy: Humanoid

Strengths: Very agile; great upper body strength

Weaknesses: Vaporization; extreme cold

Temperament: Highly aggressive

Favorite attack method: Dismemberment

Best killed by: Removing helmet, then inflicting head trauma

What the Army Doesn't Want You to Know

According to top-secret sources, some 872 drums containing contaminated zombies have been listed as "missing" by the U.S. government. Because just one drum, if opened, can cause a massive zombie outbreak, we must be on constant alert.

In the late '70s, a housing project construction crew stumbled upon a zombie burial ground, where they uncovered hundreds of still-moving heads left over from government research a decade earlier, proving once again that ignoring proper disposal methods creates a great risk.

Rob Sacchetto

Voodoo Zombie

The Voodoo Zombie is non-infectious and may be made of either live or dead flesh, depending on its stage in the "afterlife cycle." These zombies are technically not dead at all but simply buried alive in a near-death state. A potent neurotoxin is administered to the victim, causing him or her to appear dead. After a physician has mistakenly signed the death certificate, the victim is buried and later secretly exhumed by the voodoo priest to begin carrying out its master's bidding. Voodoo Zombies are used primarily as slaves and instruments of revenge. In rare cases, they have actually died and still continued to perform their tasks until complete tissue breakdown. These zombies do not pose a significant threat unless their master wishes to inflict harm. In fact, the greater danger is to be transformed into one of these zombies. The experience has been described by survivors as a waking Hell.

Distinguishing Features
- Mouth agape
- Tattered clothing
- Bad breath
- Heavily soiled clothing and skin
- Large, blank, staring eyes
- Rigid, trancelike movement

Voodoo Zombie Traits

Where found: Africa, Haiti, West Indies, Louisiana

Anatomy: Human

Strengths: Slightly stronger than humans; pain-resistant; require little sustenance

Weaknesses: Ingesting meat or salt breaks their trance

Temperament: Docile unless directed to kill, then ultra-violent

Favorite attack method: Any way commanded

Best killed by: Anything that would kill a regular human being

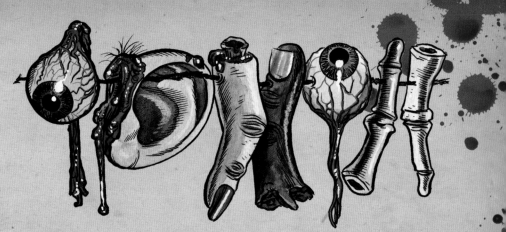

Zombie Serial Killer

In the mid-1980s, a zombie under the control of a prominent witch doctor stalked and murdered 72 people who were trying to overthrow the Haitian government. In true serial killer style, the unusually inventive zombie hid a gruesome cache of "souvenirs" from his victims—a rare case in which a Voodoo Zombie did pose a direct threat to human life. The events were chronicled in a children's skipping-rope rhyme.

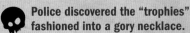 Police discovered the "trophies" fashioned into a gory necklace.

Worked Past Death

So strong was the voodoo trance over one Haitian zombie that eight months after the death of his master, he was found riddled with disease, arthritis and other ailments, still toiling in the sugar cane field he'd been ordered to maintain. It is said that when his curse was lifted, he immediately collapsed to the ground and began to decompose.

Alien-Controlled Zombies

Aliens from outer space may either control humans or snatch and inhabit their bodies. In both situations, the resulting human victim can be classified as a zombie. Luckily, in most alien-control cases, the zombie can be "cured" by finding and destroying the alien. For a live-flesh alien zombie, destroying the alien causes total memory loss of the atrocities the host has committed; for a dead-flesh alien zombie, it brings about a complete and sudden collapse. The live-flesh type usually strives to replace or control world leaders, so look for conspiracies and strange protrusions on the back of the neck. Alien-controlled dead-flesh zombies, however, are usually used as pawns in combat to soften up the human race so the aliens can take control without significant damage to cities or infrastructure. Since the aliens' ultimate goal is world domination, ACZs pose a double threat. Not only do they have to be identified and stopped, but the aliens that control them must also be neutralized.

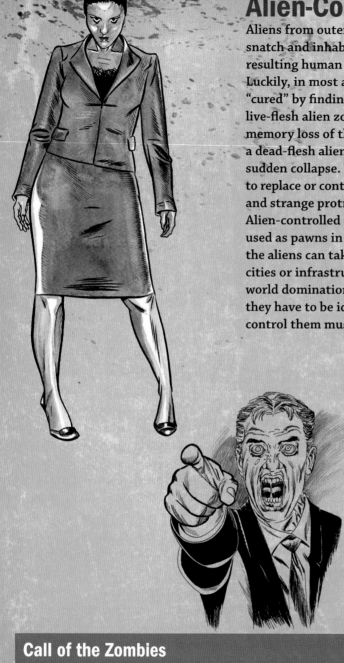

Distinguishing Features

- Blank stare
- Emotionless
- Dressed in official government attire
- Protrusion on back of neck
- Monotonic voice

Alien-Controlled Zombie Traits

Where found: Government buildings

Anatomy: Humanoid

Strengths: Hard to detect; persuasive; enhanced strength and stamina

Weaknesses: Common human frailties

Temperament: Calm, sedate and centered until summoned to kill

Favorite attack method: Sneak attack

Best killed by: Destroying the mother ship

Call of the Zombies

What makes ACZs so effective is their ability to remain undetected until they choose to reveal themselves, often by emitting a strange call from altered vocal chords, alerting others of their kind to attack.

The Controlling Device

The zombie-creating alien parasite attaches itself to a human host at the base of the skull or lower down on the back of the neck. It is deposited there by the aliens while the host is unconscious, or it is flung to its spot by another zombie. Sometimes the alien parasite drops from a high position onto an unsuspecting host. When it reaches its mark, it quickly inserts its proboscis into the brain stem and overtakes its victim, fully controlling him or her until it is removed.

Zombifying Alien Types

The following types of space aliens are known to be responsible for human zombification:

Brain slug—External attachment to host

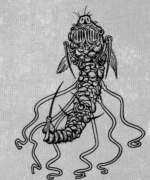

Insectaroid—Internal burrowing in host

Pod—Plant-based replicant

Starfish—External attachment to host at brain stem

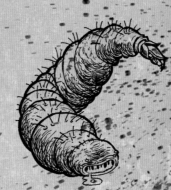

Brain worm—Burrowing into brain from the ear canal

Zombie Animals

Few animals are immune to the zombie virus. Once infected, animals grow extremely violent with bloodlust and will even endanger themselves to get to their prey. Dogs and cats may break their own bones or sever limbs to squeeze under doors, through bars and fenceposts or down ventilation shafts. When whole zoos become zombified, the ensuing violence can reach epic proportions. Whether dog or cat, elephant or ostrich, a zombie animal's reckless violence and unquenchable bloodlust makes it an even greater threat than its humanoid counterparts. It is of utmost importance to avoid contact with any zombified animal.

Distinguishing Features

- Excessive drooling or frothing from mouth
- Hoards body parts for later consumption
- Aggressive behavior in spite of wounds
- Missing or injured limbs
- Pupils no longer visible
- Acute trauma

Zombie Animal Traits

Where found: Anywhere there are animals—the great outdoors, zoos, farms

Anatomy: varied—mammalian, reptilian, amphibian, etc.

Strengths: More violent and tenacious than other animals

Weaknesses: Differ by species: cats—easily distracted by bloody ball of yarn; elephants—zombie mouse

Temperament: Frenzied

Favorite attack method: Tooth, claw, trunk, tusk, horn, etc.

Best killed by: Fire or precision nuclear strike

Carriers

The following animals do not become zombies, but can be carriers of the virus:

- Vulture
- Platypus
- Hagfish
- Komodo dragon
- Pigeon
- Lamprey

Killing Zombie Animals

Killing animals is cruel. But once infected, your pet is no longer an animal. It's a zombie and must be killed immediately. Zombie animals become so ferocious, however, that it often takes more than a single well-placed head wound to stop them. When in doubt, follow the old zombie-fighting adage: Don't stop shooting until its head is gone.

Here are some unsettling images of what it took in various instances to stop zombified beasts.

Bighorn sheep—Five shotgun blasts, six arrows

German shepherd—Four 22-caliber gunshots

Rabbit—14 pellet gunshots

Bear—17 shotgun blasts, one axe

What You Got There, Little Fella?

Sixty percent of animal zombies become zombified by eating zombie remains, so don't let your backyard get cluttered with re-killed zombies.

The Apathy Zombie

Among all the different forms of zombies, the Apathy Zombie is perhaps the least impressive. It is of the live flesh variety, but just barely. Although Apathy Zombies are found the world over, they are most heavily concentrated in the United States and Canada. They stay mostly solitary or in groups of two or three, hanging out in their parents' basements or in small, smelly apartments. Their diet consists primarily of processed foods, high in saturated fats, sodium and sugar. They are not hunters and desperately need food and drink brought to them.

Apathy Zombies often emit low moans or mumblings that, if listened to closely, sound remarkably like complaints about their lot in life or the state of the world, however absurd given their apparent lack of motivation. Smelling of human body odor, Apathy Zombies have a pale, pasty complexion and are prone to antisocial behavior. They detest natural sunlight and fresh air, and although they can travel in it, they appear considerably weakened when they do. They are quite adept at repelling the opposite sex. The best way to avoid this type of zombie is to ignore it with extreme prejudice.

Distinguishing Features

- Slouched or reclining position
- Pale skin
- Signs of acne
- Eyes half open
- Mouth agape
- Poor hygiene

Apathy Zombie Traits

Where found: Musty basements, fan conventions

Anatomy: Human

Strengths: Ability to sit for hours; gaming; computer programming

Weaknesses: Intolerance for sunlight, exercise, fresh air, and healthy eating

Temperament: Bored, despondent, tired

Favorite attack method: Insults

Best killed by: Power failure, physical labor

Foul Facts

Because of their poor diet and personal hygiene, live-flesh Apathy Zombies often emit foul odors rivaling even their dead-flesh cousins. AZs are by far the least threatening of all zombies, as simply walking away renders them ineffectual.

Harmless

More than 90 percent of all Apathy Zombies are harmless. The remaining 10 percent aren't even dangerous. They just slowly milk their parents' money while living in the basement.

Rob Sacchetto

Biblical or End of the World Zombie

Various types of walking dead have been called "End of the World Zombies," but the term is inaccurate. It's a good thing we haven't encountered real End of the World Zombies yet, because nothing can be done to save humankind from their onslaught. Based on biblical and ancient prophesies, these creatures are undoubtedly the worst, most contagious, sickening, vicious and horrific of all zombies. They simply can't be killed. They can summon demons that spring from dead flesh as they ride corpses to earth from Hell. The End of the World Zombie plague can even infect plants, turning them into poisonous monstrosities that can "walk" on their exposed roots. There is no safe place to hide when these zombies come, and no handbook can prepare you.

Distinguishing Features
- Demons visible on surface of flesh
- Horribly disfigured
- Stench of sulfur and brimstone
- Bared teeth
- Sunken, dead eyes
- Heavily mottled skin complexion

End of the World Zombie Traits
Where found: When the time comes…everywhere

Anatomy: Grotesque humanoid

Strengths: All-powerful

Weaknesses: None

Temperament: Berserk

Favorite attack method: Total obliteration

Best killed by: Not applicable

End of the World Prophecies

According to ancient texts, demons from Hell stow away in the rotting flesh of End of the World Zombies, only to pop off their cadaverous hosts at the appropriate time and embark on their own apocalyptic killing sprees.

 An artist's rendering of how demons might exit from the End of the World Zombie

The Fabled "Death Glance"

Not that EOWZs need any help killing people, but many of them are believed to possess a death glance, which can age the victim about 30 years a minute.

As the end of the world approaches, it is said, the earth will become so infected by the zombie virus that even plants and trees will feast on the living, adding yet another dimension to the horror.

Zombies vs. Mummies

Though mummies are also a species of living dead and pose a threat to humans, they differ from zombies in one essential respect: they are not contagious. You do not turn into a mummy if one bites you. Upon emerging from their tombs, mummies, like zombies, seek to harvest humans to reconstitute their emaciated forms. Mummies are easy to spot as they emerge, wrapped in gauze bandages, from their brightly colored sarcophagi. Once reanimated, they can wield curses against humankind, making them extremely dangerous. With so many ancient tombs waiting to be opened, the mummy threat remains imminent.

Zombie

Mummy

Distinguishing Mummy Features
- Decrepit appearance
- Yellow teeth
- Filthy gauze wrapping
- Stiff, rigid posture
- Skin stretched over skeletal frame
- Three-thousand-year-old morning breath

In ancient Egypt, cats stood guard over the tombs of cursed mummies, as this rendering from 2400 BCE shows. To this day, cats are still one of the most effective means by which to ward off these vengeful corpses.

When forced to retreat, the mummy can shapeshift into a sandstorm.

Zombies vs. Supermodels

Some groups of humans can be mistaken for zombies: the elderly, the homeless and especially the elderly homeless. But no group bears such an uncanny resemblance to the living dead as runway supermodels. With their emaciated bodies, pale skin and often horrendous makeup, these denizens of the catwalk have more in common with zombies than one might think. The following is a quick guide for answering the question, "Is that a supermodel or a zombie?"

Supermodel	Zombie
Favorite food: Water, laxatives, cocaine	Brains
Body type: Skeletal	Skeletal
Suffers from: Anorexia, narcissism	Everlasting death
Strengths: Sex appeal	Can eat your face
Lifespan: Four years—from 18 to 22	Indefinite

the Zombie Diet

Brain appétit

Eating Habits

Devouring humans is every zombie's purpose and passion. Scientists have sought to learn what unique attributes of this diet drive the undead to feast on the living. Their efforts to unlock the mysteries of zombie food cravings hold promise of some day controlling mass attacks by the living dead.

Brains, Brains, Brains

To a zombie, human brains are pure ambrosia. Reliable sources report that human cerebral matter provides the nutrients essential for zombies' mobility, strength and stamina. Further, it helps keep them in one piece by slowing the decay of undead flesh and organs.

Some clinical necrologists theorize that eating human brains may also take away the pain of being dead. According to this theory, brain-eating may be highly addictive, which would explain why zombies seem to attack humans so violently for the coveted substance.

Although zombies can sustain themselves on dead brain matter, they prefer the brains of living or newly deceased humans. The electrical impulses still firing through fresh brains provide an exhilarating rush to zombies' bodies and a tangy zip to their all-but-dead taste buds.

 Brains must be eaten with every meal or a zombie's body may begin to rapidly break down and whither.

Cravings and Hunger

In the mid-1990s, a group of top scientists from a major university's Department of Near-Death Phenomena won a government pork-barrel grant to perform covert experiments on a group of captive zombies. In order to learn the extent of a zombie's actual need for human brains, they gave only small portions of brain matter to one group, while another group got all the gray matter they could eat. The tests revealed that zombies actually only need about one-tenth of what they devour, but they lack any neurological trigger to feel "full." If allowed unlimited food, they will continue eating until they burst. The zombies' complete lack of control over their consumption of human brains puts them at the mercy of their own gluttony, the scientists concluded.

Arm: 3,000 calories

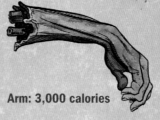

Head: 5,200 calories

Heart: 4,000 calories

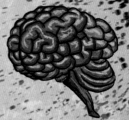

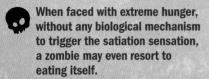

When faced with extreme hunger, without any biological mechanism to trigger the satiation sensation, a zombie may even resort to eating itself.

Brain: 5,000 calories

Rob Sacchetto

Brains

To better understand the physiological effects the consumption of brains has on zombies, and to learn where their mad desire to ingest this substance comes from, scientists carefully studied the dietary habits of a controlled group of zombies in the laboratory for several years. They discovered that the various parts of the human brain serve different mental and physical needs for zombies.

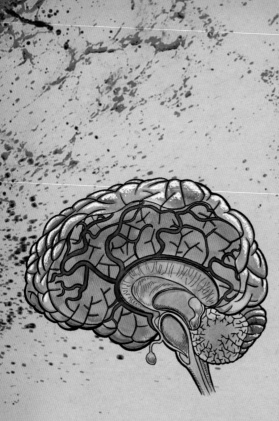

Cerebral cortex—Eaten in large enough quantities, the brain cells of the human cerebrum help zombies learn from their mistakes—for instance, "fire" equals "bad." This food comprises the entire outer covering of the brain and can therefore be eaten in great quantities.

Cerebellum—When a zombie eats this part of the brain, it experiences a calm, satiated state. Although difficult to get to, the cerebellum is well worth the effort because of its calming effects.

Hypothalamus—This revered part of the brain fulfills zombies' craving for salt and aids in absorbing nutrients that keep their rotting flesh soft and supple. A depletion of hypothalamus cells in their diet makes zombies highly irritable.

Olfactory bulb—The olfactory bulb provides the walking dead with a keen brain-smelling sense to better search out future meals.

Medulla oblongata—Eating this portion of the brain stem helps keep zombies moving by improving reflexes, alertness and digestion. Such improvements help zombies transcend their corpselike states and move more fluidly.

Pons—This part of the lower brain gives zombies short bursts of increased strength.

Brain Eating Record

In 1983, a zombie in Hackensack, NJ cornered an auditorium full of middle schoolers and devoured more than 90 brains, a world record for a single sitting. The zombie's stomach exploded shortly thereafter.

Effects of a No-Brain Diet

When a zombie cannot get fresh human brains to eat, it quickly becomes emaciated and sickly, its body rotting ever more quickly until there is little left but a quivering mass of goo. The first thing to decompose is the zombie's eyes, which rapidly begin to liquefy and leak out of their sockets. Such zombies, though slow and sickly, are crazed with hunger and will attack anything in their paths. Approach with extreme caution.

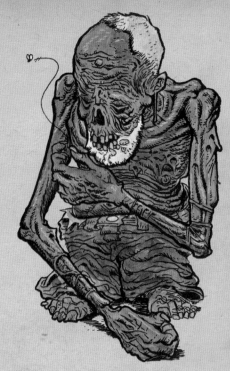

💀 **A zombie on a brainless diet**

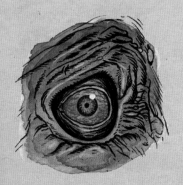

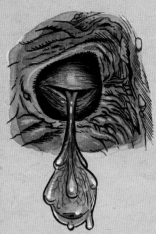

💀 In the top image we have a close-up of a healthy zombie eye. Beneath it, a zombie eye after eight days without brains.

In rare cases, some of the living dead have been observed hoarding brain matter for later consumption.

Zombie Food Pyramid

Brains are not the only source of nutrients a zombie craves and consumes. Scientists studying the zombie diet have compiled the following Food Pyramid:

Eyeballs, fingers, toes, etc.

For a zombie, small body parts are the equivalent of a bowl of cheese puffs. Although they may taste great, they offer very little in the form of nutrition and should be considered a snack only.

Intestines

Although they have some nutritional value, eating guts tends to make a zombie fussy, bloated and lethargic. Like a giant bowl of spaghetti and meatballs for humans, intestines are easy to eat but don't offer much nutrition for zombies.

Heart

Though difficult to access and tough to chew, the heart does offer a broad spectrum of zombie-sustaining nutrients and should be eaten whenever available.

Essential organs

The liver, pancreas, kidneys, lungs and other vital human organs offer a zombie many nourishing properties and should be eaten as often as possible. When a swarm of zombies feeds on one human, it may be hard for all of them to get shares of these essential organs.

The brain

This pinnacle of zombie nutrition must be consumed as often as possible. It contains a virtual cornucopia of zombie-sustaining elements, aiding longevity and pain relief. Zombies stop at nothing to get this most essential food.

Cuts of Meat

Experts often find it necessary to imagine, based on research, how a zombie may view humans. Just as a butcher may look at an animal and visualize how it can be divided into various cuts of meat, so too may a zombie view human flesh.

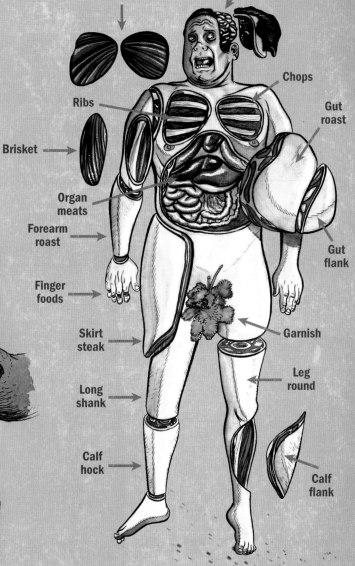

Upper-body chuck

Brain panzarotti

Chops

Ribs

Gut roast

Brisket

Organ meats

Forearm roast

Gut flank

Finger foods

Garnish

Skirt steak

Leg round

Long shank

Calf hock

Calf flank

Human Cuts of Meat Chart

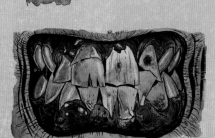

Butchering Instruments

Teeth and claws, made jagged through decay, aid zombies in tearing through flesh.

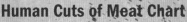

Zombie Food-Combining Diet

By studying zombies' brain chemistry while eating, researchers have shed light on how the undead regard the taste of various human body parts. Their research shows that zombies eagerly seek out those body parts that most physically empower them and, interestingly, those that offer flavors and textures reminiscent of their living past. Often, zombies will combine certain body parts to get the maximum nutritional and/or taste benefits of their meal, much the way ancient Mesoamerican peoples combined corn and beans to maximize each ingredient's full dietary benefits.

Food Combination	Tastes Like	Effect on Zombies
1: Eyeballs, liver	Lamb chops	Helps stamina
2: Kidney, spinal fluid	Dr. Pepper	Relieves joint atrophy
3: Frontal lobe, bladder	Chocolate-covered hazelnuts	Improves brain-finding, relieves death pain
4: Brain stem, urethra	Cashews	Maintains glossy coat and fights tooth decay
5: Lungs, cerebral cortex	Rare steak and mushrooms	Keeps the bugs off
6: Eyeballs, kidney	Oysters Rockefeller	Prevents sluggishness
7: Stomach lining, esophagus	Grilled salmon	Acts as an antifreeze
8: Large intestine, duodenum	French fries	Slightly curbs appetite
9: Tongue, anus	Turkey potpie	Masks "death breath" with "ass breath"
10: Heart, inner ear	Strawberry sorbet	Increases ferocity

Zombie Hydration

Although zombies do not need to drink human blood to survive, the way that vampires do, they swallow it gratuitously and in great quantities to aid esophageal lubrication and digestion.

Ideally, a zombie will drink at least eight cups of blood per day to maximize digestive efficiency. Those who drink less tend to be irritable, sluggish and irregular in their bowel movements.

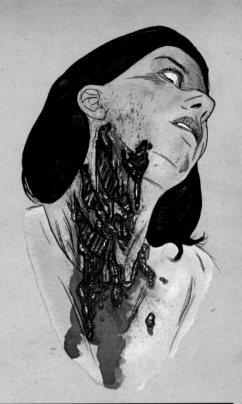

Blood Inc.

In a new pilot program, government-backed companies have begun to distribute blood from natural casualties to zombies, hoping to reduce their violence toward live humans.

Nutrition Facts

Serving Size 12 fl. oz (360 ml)

Amount per serving		
Calories 1200		**Calories from fat** 820
		% Daily Value*
Total Fat 76g		166%
Saturated Fat 55g		155%
Trans Fat 21g		112%
Cholesterol 326mg		128%
Sodium 3000mg		140%
Total Carbohydrate 12g		4%
Dietary Fiber 0g		0%
Sugars 70g		
Protein 127g		
Vitamin A 76%	Vitamin C	4%
Calcium 81%	Iron	300%

*Percent Daily Values are based on a 2,000 calorie diet

Zombie Digestion

It remains unclear how zombies actually metabolize the materials they ingest. Close observation on controlled zombie groups has concluded that actual absorption and utilization of nutrients does occur even though zombies cannot fully break down hard waste. The most notable trait of the zombie digestive system is its expanded stomach, four times the size of a normal human stomach.

 The zombie digestive tract: Notice how the stomach has pushed aside all other organs, including the lungs.

Some experts hypothesize that zombies may produce enzymes not found in the human body that extract nourishment while leaving food mostly undigested. But so far no specialized or evolved enzyme has been found to prove this theory, even after extensive forensic studies of zombies' internal organs and waste material.

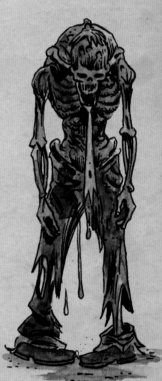

 Zombie food (before and after digestion)

Zombie Indigestion

A zombie's inability to break down hard waste is a great disadvantage that may lead to lasting physical damage. Zombies apparently expel waste in three ways: spectacular projectile vomiting, a bursting of matter directly from the torso and the traditional human fecal method.

These observations further point to the enzyme theory. After nutrients are extracted from human body parts, the hard waste remains and cannot be broken down enough to be evacuated from the undead body by normal means.

After years of research on zombie digestion, observation of captive zombies and continued research efforts, scientists believe they may be close to finding a way to utilize the mystery enzyme in an effort to stop zombies from destroying mankind.

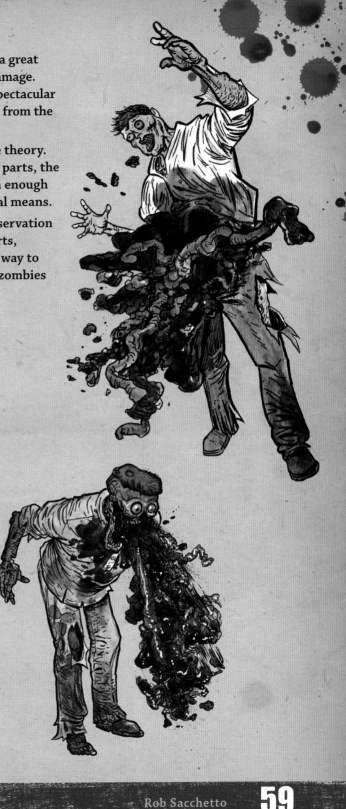

Zombie
Life

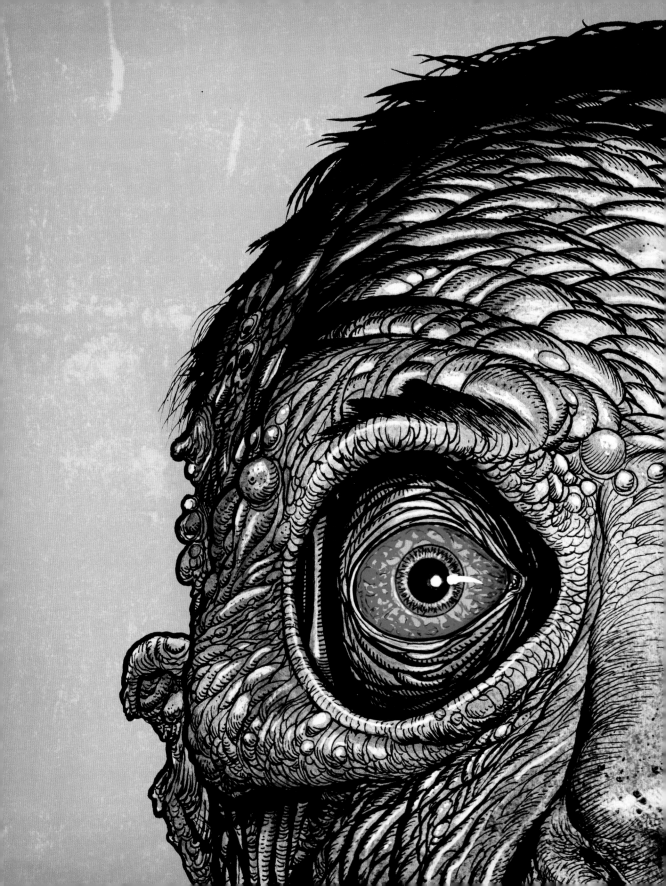

Understanding Zombie Life

Acquiring food is the most basic instinct for these flesh-eaters.

The more you understand zombie "life," the more prepared you will be to meet the challenges of the coming Zombie Apocalypse. Knowing details about their habits and capabilities will help you in either exterminating them or dealing with a forced coexistence. Although they are not motivated by what humans recognize as emotions, zombies exhibit a myriad of other humanlike behaviors. They are primarily driven by basic survival instincts, including food, shelter (to a lesser degree) and, in rare instances, even procreation.

Much of what is known about zombies today comes from the research of Rosalyn Brown, a noted zombiologist and photographer who spent years tracking zombie outbreaks. Her groundbreaking work forms the backbone of modern zombiology.

"In order for me to study zombies for so long, I had to remember that, despite their appearance, zombies are no longer human. Secondly, I had to understand that because their prey is human, I was not only putting myself in grave danger, but I had to objectively witness and document many human casualties. These proved to be the most difficult tasks, but by doing so I feel that I have served a greater good."

— Rosalyn Brown

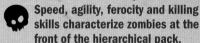

Speed, agility, ferocity and killing skills characterize zombies at the front of the hierarchical pack.

Zombie Hierarchy

There is a hierarchy in the zombie world. For the most part, Recently Dead Zombies (RDZs) lead attacks, while their slower, less mobile counterparts, the Exhumed Corpse Zombies (ECZs), bring up the rear, scavenging for leftovers. It may be that RDZs are simply faster, or perhaps—as in animal and human societies—the weaker members of the species naturally follow their leaders, who are generally the strongest in a group.

Ten Zombie Facts

1. Not all zombies are slow.
2. Many zombies do not require brains to "live."
3. Zombies cannot function in freezing temperatures.
4. The best way to kill a zombie is with a gunshot to the head.
5. Zombies abound in Haiti.
6. Zombies see dead people.
7. Some zombies retain their ability to speak.
8. Zombies hate stairs.
9. The government is secretly working to create a zombie army.
10. Zombies are coming to get you.

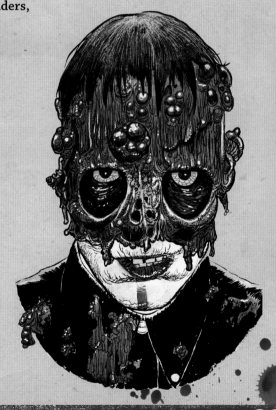

Rob Sacchetto

Zombie Habitat

During outbreaks, zombies have been seen in a wide variety of habitats. Some lead an entirely outdoor life. Others take up residence in cellars, caves or subway tunnels. They seem to be at home anywhere they can find sustenance, a necessary adaptive skill for creatures so compelled to feed on living flesh.

Proper hygiene is not a consideration in the zombie home.

Prefer darker, shadowy areas

Storage of food

Smashing block

Zombies use hammers and other implements to smash food so it can be digested more easily.

Bones smashed for marrow

Overcrowding

Despite a massive influx of zombies gathering to search for food in a given area, overcrowding does not result in the same problems it would for humans. Zombies seem quite indifferent to standing shoulder-to-shoulder for long periods of time, a condition to which many humans have a serious aversion.

 Overcrowding in the zombie world is not viewed as a problem.

The Zombie Home

Some zombies make temporary shelters in urban areas, where prey is more plentiful. They prefer darker alleys, subways, tunnels, spaces under bridges and any place unsuspecting humans are likely to hide.

Migration

Zombies lead a nomadic life, constantly moving from place to place in search of food. Some stop briefly to break their prey down for further consumption. One factor that keeps zombies on the move is below-freezing temperatures, which force them away from northern areas for part of the year. The end of summer sees a massive southward migration of zombies. As luck would have it, in winter most human prey vacations in zombie migration areas.

Shown here is a vast migrating herd, or "strangle," of zombies.

Rob Sacchetto

A zombie attacks a human female for mating purposes.

Zombie Mating Habits

The details of zombie mating have been among the most important revelations in researching the living dead. Although dead, zombie males can actually impregnate both living and "undead" females. A Recently Dead Zombie male reaches its sexual peak within six months of reanimation. Unlike human gestation, which takes nine full months, zombie gestation takes only a few weeks. To control mass panic, this information has long been kept from public perception of how new zombies are created.

Mammalian-style sexual activity, or "rutting," can occur at any time with any partner—living, dead, or living dead. Zombies are not very particular about who, or even what, their partners are. Once you're a zombie, anything goes. There is no courtship in the world of the undead, as the need to feel personal involvement, commitment or any other human emotion no longer exists.

A potential partner for the rutting zombie

Zombie Copulation

When it comes to mating, there is no zombie "love," just straightforward, mechanical sexual relations for the purpose of procreation. The living dead can be quite creative in their attempts, though, due to their varying states of decay, which force them to adopt a wide variety of sexual positions and styles.

Viewers beware. The following images are of an extremely graphic nature and should not be viewed by the squeamish, easily embarrassed, or those with heart trouble.

The legless donkey

The triple dipper

The dinner belle

The typical zombie family has no genetic relationship, although it may come together to superficially resemble a traditional human family unit.

The Zombie Family

A zombie "family" may come together and function as a unit for brief periods of time. When it is time to migrate, however, they will split up and go their separate ways. Very few zombies are ever seen together twice. Since zombies have no social connections or memories of their own families, what appears to be a close-knit family group may be simply a bunch of unrelated zombies interacting with each other, usually for hunting.

Indifference

Zombies are altogether devoid of human emotion and attachment. There is no zombie love, hate, passion or longing. This makes them almost perfect killing machines. Their angry appearance stems from a constant, painful hunger.

While the traditional family unit does not exist for zombies, zombie children can sometimes be seen acting out "playful" behavior while adult zombies seem to supervise.

Zombie Babies

Zombie copulation can occasionally result in living-dead offspring. Never underestimate the ferocity of these infant zombies. After a zombie baby has ripped its way out of its mother's torso with a bloodcurdling cry, it will proceed to devour her and may even call others to come feed.

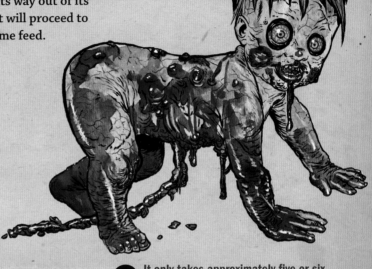

 It only takes approximately five or six zombie "children" to strip a corpse completely to the bone.

Zombie babies develop much more quickly than their human counterparts. Within one week of their birth, they begin to seek out toys—primarily dolls—that will aid in developing their ability to kill. Even at this tender age, they are already hardwired for homicide.

 Toys aid in the development of zombie babies' manual dexterity for killing.

Zombie Religion

Zombie "death" invites thoughtful speculation about such questions as whether there is an afterlife for zombies and whether a murder committed by a zombie should be considered a crime against God.

Although zombies have been known to congregate in and around churches, synagogues, and temples, it seems that they do so only when there are people barricaded inside. It is difficult to know how, if at all, the undead regard religion. Most experts believe that for zombies, religion gets in the way of hunting, killing and eating, so it is irrelevant to their existence.

Before or immediately after fully becoming zombies, some individuals have been observed to commit zombie suicide, perhaps to avoid killing and eating others, which suggests that, early in their transformation, zombies may actually have vestiges of conscious thought. But once a zombie has passed from life to death and back to living death, any remnants of conscience, morals, or spirituality are long gone. All that remains is a hungry, godless, rotting shell.

 Is there a place in heaven for zombies?

Zombie Politics

Research has yielded fascinating insight into the world of zombie politics. There are no elections in the zombie world, but there is a political hierarchy. That hierarchy is ascended by simply being the strongest and most brutal of zombies. Human political concepts are rendered useless in the walking afterlife; success in the zombie world is measured by what one can provide. One who can lead a swarm to new sources of brains and live flesh is regarded as superior among the zombie ranks, and will quickly become their leader.

Zombies, like the zombie virus itself, are constantly in a state of evolutionary flux. Some advance, adapting to their environment or needs, while others decline. Each new batch of zombies exhibits different traits. Such environmental adaptation has caused more advanced "alpha zombies" to evolve.

These zombie leaders show signs of forward thinking, going so far as to develop strategies in warfare against humans. They will send long-dead zombies and Exhumed Corpse Zombies as pawns in potentially lethal situations. They may also oversee food dismemberment and distribution among followers. Life at the head of the pack is not all peaches and cream, however. Zombie leaders can be overthrown by younger, stronger, and more ambitious newly-turned zombies. The loser of these coups is eaten.

 Pictured here is the super-alpha zombie. A mutated creature, it is highly evolved, bigger, stronger and faster than its counterparts and possessed of the ability to wield crude weapons.

 Zombie evolution may one day lead to refined political tactics that mirror our own.

Rob Sacchetto

Zombie Behavior

Although zombies spend the majority of their time feeding, they may occasionally dabble in the pursuits of their former daily lives—a sign of behavioral imprinting on their brains. They seem to act out these behaviors in a completely mechanical way, with only habit to guide them.

Because they are imprinted with repetitive actions from their former lives, when zombies are temporarily satiated, they involuntarily revert to these behaviors. As their brains continue to deteriorate, however, even these actions will stop and the zombies will stumble around aimlessly.

 A zombie whom we can assume was once a human teacher conducts nonexistent students in an abandoned classroom.

Once high-powered businessmen, these zombies habitually interact in macabre power meetings.

Proof of zombies' adherence to routine: A repeat offender in his former life, this zombie continued to rob banks even though he no longer had any use for money.

Zombie Leisure

Unlike their routine behavior, some zombies seem to genuinely immerse themselves and even show signs of concentration in what can be described as leisure activities, though they derive no pleasure that way. One captive zombie, a golfer in his previous life, was observed carefully putting an eyeball into a hole with much effort.

In another instance, researchers watched a female zombie walking a dog for several miles without resorting to violence or eating the mutt. She later simply let go of the leash and let the dog escape unharmed as she resumed her hunt for food. Though zombies can show seemingly human characteristics, bear in mind that these killing machines will always return to their basic need to feed.

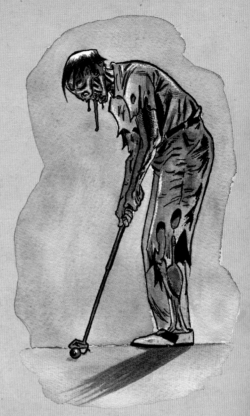

💀 Zombies are no less deadly when seemingly engaged in leisure pursuits.

💀 Although diverted for a brief time, the zombie will soon return to feeding.

Surviving
the
Zombie Apocalypse

Surviving the Apocalypse

This chapter will prepare you for the war against the enemy. You will learn such useful tactics as how to escape from zombies, how to make effective weapons from ordinary household items and how to zombie-proof your home in preparation for an impending Apocalypse. Memorize these skills. Your life depends upon it.

Much of the information in this chapter was furnished by Colonel Montgomery Haardash, the world's foremost authority on zombie warfare. A veteran of hundreds of secret head-on battles against zombies, Colonel Haardash has received countless medals and awards, including the coveted "Ultimate Survivalist" award from *Soldier of Fortune* magazine, and has devoted his life to stopping the Zombie Apocalypse.

Fitness for Zombie Hunters

The number one weapon against the zombie enemy is your body. You must be in peak physical condition on the battlefield. Ideally, you will be able to find shelter to avoid the zombie hordes altogether, but if you have no cover, you'll either have to run or engage the enemy in physical combat.

Upper body strength is immensely important when inflicting the head trauma necessary to stop a zombie. Since zombies usually come in swarms, you will need endurance as well as brute force. An effective way to work on the appropriate muscle groups is to spend an hour a day taking a sledgehammer to a big rig tire.

In case you need to fight the enemy with a gun, make sure your trigger finger won't cramp up on you when you need it most. When facing large numbers of zombies, you will have to fire multiple times to clear a way through. Tying a weight or heavy stone to your finger for pull-ups is a good way to gain manual strength and endurance.

She may look like your grandma, but she's not. Escape immediately.

Escaping from Zombies

Even if you have molded your body into prime physical condition, you must learn how to evade the enemy. This is the only viable strategy when confronted by the sheer number of zombies that will be spawned in an outbreak. Here are the most important points to know when trying to escape zombies' persistent attempts to eat you.

1. Don't walk. Run. You don't want to buy into the myth that zombies are slow-moving automatons.

2. Establish yourself on middle ground. Do not hole up in a highrise or subway tunnel, where you would be cutting yourself off from the necessities for life.

3. If you find yourself trapped in a highrise building, don't use the elevator. You do not want to risk stopping at a floor full of zombies who have been pushing that button all day.

4. Find shelter that provides the essentials—food, water, weapons and medical supplies. One of the best places to hole up is your local convenience store.

5. Trust no one. Although some zombies may look humanlike, they are not. Even cherished loved ones, once transformed, will want to eat your brains.

Stairs

Although zombies can climb stairs, like many humans, they avoid doing so unless absolutely necessary. For that reason, stairways can provide temporary shelter when escaping from zombies.

Find the Cold

Get as far away from the equator as possible. One thing zombies can't handle is extreme cold. Zombies have no way of naturally heating their bodies, so in sub-zero temperatures they move more and more slowly until they seize up completely. In this frozen state, they are completely helpless, and all you have to do is separate the head from the body.

 Don't wait for the spring thaw. Decapitate as soon as possible.

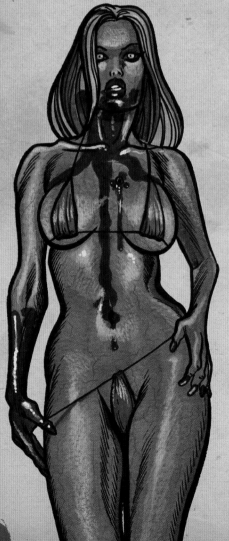

Avoid the Enticing Zombie

Not all zombies appear rotten and festering. A zombie bikini model may come on to you—but remember, she only wants you for your brain. Be prepared to run or blow her head off. The mistaken belief that the living dead are still human has cost many lives. Once identification has been confirmed, do not hesitate for even a moment before destroying them.

Zombie Weaknesses

Being undead and all, zombies are notoriously hard to kill. But they do have weaknesses. The trick is in knowing what those weaknesses are and how to exploit them.

Head Trauma

The best way to stop a zombie is to shoot it in the head or sever its head completely. In fact, any severe head trauma may render the zombie completely inactive. But both shooting and severing the head have drawbacks. Shooting means you will likely need an infinite supply of bullets to fight off the sheer number of zombies. Severing the head forces you to get up-close and personal. This is why it's always handy to have both weapons at your side.

Bullet Wounds

Putting bullets through crucial joints can be effective. The walking dead cannot feel pain, but they won't be able to use a limb that has an incapacitated joint. Drawback: You must be extremely accurate.

Severed Limbs

Severing a limb is much more effective than shooting a joint. If you cut off a zombie's legs, it cannot chase you. Severing its arms means it can't grab you. Note: Severing one leg is actually better than severing both, as the zombie will stumble around in a circle while you escape. Drawback: You have to get damn close to a zombie to chop part of it off.

Sound Waves

As certain sound vibrations shatter crystal, so particular sound waves have been effectively used to neutralize zombies. A specific pitch can blow out a zombie's eardrums, resulting in head trauma. Drawback: A sound that blows out a zombie's eardrums will probably do the same to you. You'll need protective ear guards to avoid damaging yourself.

Eardrums bursting from sound waves

Crushing

Dropping large boulders or other items on a zombie may not entirely kill it but will certainly stop its rampage. Drawback: It takes several strong people to lift or push a large boulder—not an option when you're by yourself.

Crushing zombies is another effective way to neutralize them.

Microwave Technology

The military has been working on long-range microwave technology for weapons use. Tests on zombies have met with great success. Drawback: Only the government has access to this high-tech, experimental weaponry.

The effects of long-range microwave weapons on zombies

Hand-to-Hand Combat

Getting into a fistfight with one of the walking dead is the last thing you ever want to do. If you absolutely cannot avoid such a confrontation, do not under any circumstances punch it with bare fists. Any skin-to-skin contact may transfer the virus to you, so don't try any chokeholds or nerve pinches, and don't try to stop air or blood flow. Wrestling or grappling moves are ineffectual and will also put you at risk of a lethal fluid exchange. If you have to fight one and you've been trained in hand-to-hand zombie combat, make sure you've got your zombie-punching gloves on.

The Proper Zombie Punch

The proper zombie punch should be administered with great force under the chin so that the ghoul's brain is forced upward through its skull. Only deliver this punch while wearing special zombie-punching gloves.

The Zombie-Punching Glove

The perfect zombie-punching glove has a Teflon-nylon blended weave, non-stick knuckle protectors, forearm garter and an impermeable rubber inner coating to ensure against virus exposure.

Choosing Your Weapon

Long-range weapons are best for killing zombies outdoors. These include guns of all kinds, bows and arrows, acid sprayers, crossbows, rocket launchers and anything else that can hit a zombie hard from a distance. Keeping your distance from the infected creatures is the best way to prevent even the smallest amount of the zombie virus from entering your bloodstream. Hollow-point or explosive bullets take out the most flesh, and you don't have to be a great marksman. Remember, the bigger the bullet, the more it will incapacitate the zombie.

An acid spray canister can be a great defense against zombies.

A Bit About Blades

A blade can be an effective tool for fighting against zombies. Best of all, blades don't need reloading. Once your ammunition is gone, your gun is as effective as a ham sandwich. It's best to always carry a machete, a long-handled cleaver, an axe or some other sharp-edged tool as backup. A long handle lets you keep a safe distance from the head wound you are about to inflict.

Improvised Weapons

If a zombie catches you unaware and there is no gun shop or sporting goods store nearby, you'll need to be quick to improvise a weapon. When improvising, remember a few keys: Anything that can take off a zombie head is a good weapon. Anything that can do so at a distance is a great weapon. To use electrical weapons, you'll need to carry a power source such as a backpack generator or battery pack.

Homemade Weapons

Here are some great ideas to get you started on creating your own zombie weapons.

- Weed-wacker fitted with steak knives
- Umbrella outfitted with a screwdriver
- Walking stick or curtain rod with a blender on the end of it
- Power drill duct-taped to a coat rack or broom handle
- Five-inch nails driven through a baseball bat
- Nine-iron golf club charged with car batteries (don't forget your rubber gloves)
- Lawnmower with a shoulder strap
- Nail gun to nail a zombie in the head or board up windows in an attack
- Broken bottle fitted at the end of a pool cue
- Projectile slingshot made with elastic bands or bungee cords

A prime example of why you should not use fire against zombies at close range

Fire Weapons

Flame throwers work great, but only if you use them from behind a zombie-proof barrier. Do not use torches or other fire weapons in close quarters. A non-flaming zombie is bad enough, but you do not want an angry fireball coming for your brain. Exploding propane tanks or Molotov cocktails are only useful from a distance, because it takes precious time to completely incinerate a zombie.

Molotov cocktails: use only from a safe distance

Weapon Effectiveness

This section will illustrate the sort of damage that various weapons inflict and help to desensitize you to the atrocities you will witness in a zombie war. For an apples-to-apples comparison, each weapon has been tested on a zombie's head.

Uzi

For those who aren't great shots, the rapid firepower of the Uzi should render a zombie immobile.

Shotgun

A shotgun, properly aimed, will take out the entire back of the zombie's head, brain included.

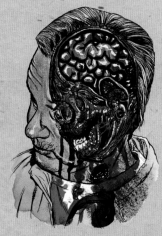

Machete

The chopping action of a machete is effective for taking out large parts of the zombie's head. The long blade keeps you at a safe distance.

Meat cleaver

A cleaver gives you the chopping depth needed to reach the zombie's brain.

Golf club

It may take a few whacks, but a sturdy nine iron makes an effective head-basher.

Rolling pin

Rolling pins require skill in fighting at close quarters and should only be used by advanced zombie warriors.

Fire

Flames can be a potent weapon, though it does take some time to burn the zombie thoroughly enough to halt its attack.

Acid

In strong doses, acid will melt a zombie into a puddle, but it may take a while, so aim for the legs first.

Handgun

Handguns work great, but only if your aim is great. Use one in case of close-quarters confrontation. At a distance, you'll waste too many bullets.

Grenade

The grenade is a powerful zombie deterrent. Just make sure you're far enough away from the explosion so you don't get covered with its infected bodily fluids.

Choosing Your Armor

Protective body covering must be impervious to bites, scratches and fluid spray. You'll also need a breathing apparatus to avoid inhaling burning zombie ash, which can carry the zombie virus. Eye protection is important, too, because tear ducts can carry zombie germs into your body. A heavy cotton-nylon fabric with strategically placed body armor similar to that worn by SWAT team personnel is ideal. Waterproof all-terrain boots make good footwear. Be sure the fit is perfect—you'll likely be doing a lot of running. Keep your head safe at all times with a double-thick helmet that repels both zombie teeth and bullets, in case fellow zombie fighters mistake you for one of the living dead. The ideal zombie-hunting uniform is the Zombie-Buster Suit.

Zombie-Buster Suit

- Global communications system
- Infrared night-motion vision and eye protection
- Face shield and breathing apparatus
- Body armor
- Breathable Teflon-coated nylon outerwear
- Side pockets for flash grenades
- Provisions
- Fully automatic 2,000-round-capacity firearm with laser sight
- 2.5-foot machete with tri-point blade and hand protection
- Mini grenades
- Steel-toe boots with shin and calf protectors
- Acid bombs that emit corrosive gas

The Zombie-Buster helmet comes with night vision and is bite-resistant up to 600 pounds of pressure per square inch.

The best zombie-killing sidearms are fully automatic, fire at least five rounds per second and are equipped with laser aiming devices.

Zombie armor comes standard with a stainless steel, never-dull machete forged for maximum decapitation abilities.

Armor Testing

The armor of the Zombie-Buster Suit was tested against enraged zombies to make sure it could withstand even the most ferocious attacks. The researchers first provoked the zombies, then presented them with various pieces of the Zombie-Buster Suit covered in brain matter to make them more appetizing.

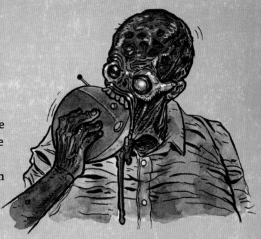

Zombie attempting to bite through Zombie-Buster helmet in testing trial

Zombie armor test phase—testing body armor against zombie bite

Zombie kicked in groin with Zombie-Buster boot in trials

Planning Your Attack

Follow the reconnaissance steps below when mapping out your attack. Failure to properly plan all aspects of your attack will leave you vulnerable to surprise. There will be no margin for error when the Zombie Apocalypse comes.

Gather information.

- Send out recon teams.
- Be sure each team is equipped with a camera, pad and pencil.
- Be in constant radio contact with your recon team.
- Locate weak spots in local surroundings, i.e., places zombies can easily infiltrate, such as manholes, swamps and dense brush.
- Locate fuel, medical, food and water supplies.
- Locate escape routes.
- Establish where the enemy has been spotted.

Choose your terrain.

- Pick high vantage points so you can spot the approaching enemy at a distance.
- Do not allow yourself to be backed into open water, the edge of a high cliff or the top of a high building.
- Do not allow zombies to trap you in dense brush, a blind alley or an underground facility such as a subway or mineshaft.
- Make your base of operations a highly fortifiable one close to escape routes and plenty of supplies, and make sure it is sizeable enough to house Apocalypse survivors comfortably.

Plan your attack.

- Lure zombies into wide open spaces, e.g., farmers' fields, landing strips, city streets or rock quarries.
- Lure zombies to the edge of high cliffs.
- Attempt to lure zombies close together for more effective use of high explosives.

Slaughter zombies.

Once you've lured a swarm of zombies into a wide open area, it's time for the slaughter. Preset land mines can be an effective tool in open spaces, where you can keep your distance from explosive splatter. Open spaces are also good for using other weapons, such as grenades, rocket launchers and fire.

The Zombie-Hunting Game

Designate point values for hitting different parts of zombie bodies. See how many points you can rack up. Legs are worth 20 points, arms and torso 10, and the headshot 50. The highest score wins. For experts: Deduct 10 points for every extra shot taken.

Make a Terrain Map

Draw up a map of your immediate area based on the information you've gathered in your reconnaissance. This terrain map will help you plan your attack, keep you safely barricaded and, if all else fails, aid you in your escape.

 A good map will aid you in luring, attacking, hiding from and escaping zombies.

Our local zombie map

The map should:

- Cover a 6-to-10 block radius
- Designate escape routes
- Show areas where zombies have been seen
- Show where traps and barricades are set up
- Show trails and alternate access routes
- Designate lookout points
- Show supply outposts, e.g., gas, medical supplies, food, weapons and tools
- Show directions zombies are traveling

The Brain Lure

Luring and Trapping Zombies

In the war against zombies, it is often necessary to inflict maximum damage, ensuring a state of superdeath for these already-dead creatures. Zombies possess little or no cerebral intelligence, so luring them into traps for extermination can be simple.

Large animal traps, such as bear traps, are effective but not fool-proof ways to capture zombies. The undead can escape these devices by severing their own limbs without losing their ability to attack you.

Luring zombies to the edge of a tall cliff and pushing them off is an effective way to end their existence. To avoid physical contact with them, use long poles to do the pushing. Pull a human brain along the ground with rope as bait, leading right up to the edge of the cliff. Then a simple poke to the head or chest is usually enough to send them careening over the side. Being pushed off a cliff may not always kill zombies, but it will at least reduce them to a mashed-up pile of twitching torsos.

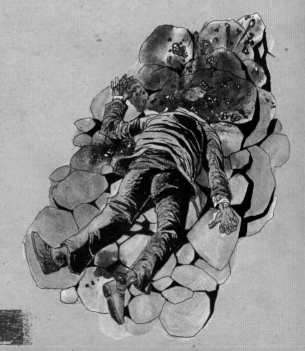

WATCH FOR FALLING ZOMBIES

Zombie Pits

The best traps are those that capture zombies in a large pit, which should be deep and big enough for several zombies—about 15 feet deep, 30 to 40 feet wide and 40 to 50 feet long. When enough zombies have fallen into the pit, there are numerous ways to dispatch them. Mowing them down with a machine gun is effective but messy. Setting fire to them works well as long as you have a special breathing apparatus: Simply drench the zombies in flammable liquid and light a match. Bathing them in acid is by far the most thoroughly destructive method. Within a couple of hours you will have a clean pit ready for more zombies.

The mother of all zombie traps: the acid pit

Before

Zombie-Proofing Your Home

When the war against zombies comes, you're going to need an operations base from which to plan your attacks. And you better make sure that your base is secure. For most people, their base will be their home. Zombie-proof it with the following steps.

Set up a perimeter.
A moat at least 30 feet deep works well. Fill it with carbolic acid instead of water, or add schools of piranhas.

Make an escape plan.
You can't live in a panic room forever. If zombies do get into your house, you'll want an underground tunnel. Make sure it leads to an even safer location.

Install an incinerator.
You don't want to chance being eaten while taking out the garbage, so burn it. You can also incinerate any people in your home who may become infected. Dead decaying bodies can really build up, but ashes just blow away in the wind.

Build a bomb shelter.
Zombies may not be your only problem. If the military decides to blast the planet's surface with a nuclear bomb, you'll need to hole up for a while. Make sure your shelter can stand up to at least a 10-megaton blast.

Stockpile ordnance.
Stockpile enough weapons and ammo to outfit a small army.

Zombie-Proofing Checklist

In a war against zombies, it is important to make provisions and fortify yourself before engaging the enemy. Make sure you've addressed each of these areas:

- Electrified fence—At least 40 feet high. Don't bother with barbed wire—you'll just have to clean off the chunks.
- Windows—The sliding, bulletproof, Lucite kind. Zombies can easily smash through regular glass.
- Electrical generator—You'll need power when the grid goes down.
- Non-perishable food—The local supermarket isn't going to be open.
- Bottled water or water purifier—The water supply will quickly become tainted.
- Brick exterior—Zombies can tear through wood and stucco.
- Astroturf lawn—Stays green even when piled with corpses.
- Acid-spraying hose—Don't waste your bullets.

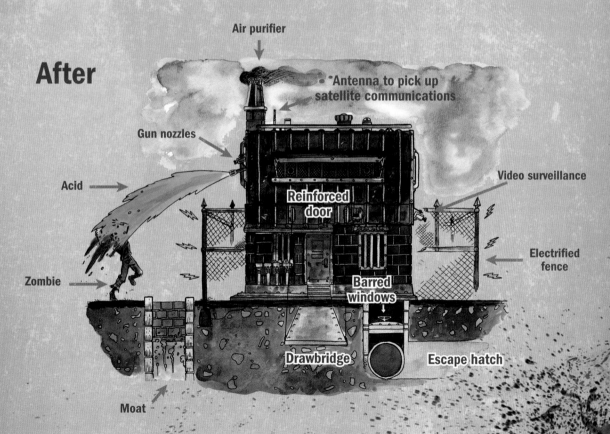

After

Air purifier

Antenna to pick up satellite communications

Gun nozzles

Acid

Video surveillance

Reinforced door

Zombie

Electrified fence

Barred windows

Drawbridge

Escape hatch

Moat

Zombie First Aid

If you have been infected by a zombie despite the preventative measures in this book, you don't need a crystal ball to predict that a gunshot to your head is in your future. But if acted on quickly enough, before the virus has entered your main bloodstream, you can treat a bite to the arm or leg by quickly and cleanly severing the appendage at the nearest joint.

With other wounds, you are out of luck. A zombie antivenom is being developed but may not be available in time to be of any use to you. The best thing to do for victims who have been bitten by a zombie is to lay them down comfortably, cover them with a soft warm blanket, offer them a cup of cocoa or glass of warm milk, use soothing words—and then deliver a head wound so severe that it pops their eyeballs from their sockets.

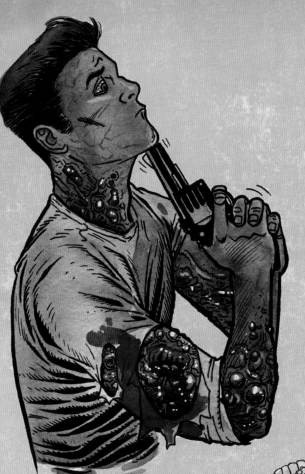

Administering Your Own First Aid

Should you become infected, the best means of killing yourself is a bullet to the head. If you do not have ready access to a gun, you may have to resort to a slower, more painful method of self-inflicted head trauma, such as running a stick through your head. Massive head trauma kills both humans and zombies.

 Proper placement of your firearm will ensure maximum brain matter destruction.

 A sharp stick driven into the head is another effective way to deal with infection. Twist it around repeatedly until the brain is scrambled.

Our Zombies, Ourselves

Can We Coexist?

By this point, you have a solid understanding of the makeup of the living dead and of what to do when the zombie outbreak finally comes. But it is also important to think about the possibility that humans and zombies may one day come to inhabit this planet together.

 Could peaceful coexistence between humans and zombies one day become a reality?

With all the similarities between humans and the reanimated dead, you might think we could learn to coexist with these carnivorous creatures. Both humans and zombies have been known to shamble aimlessly through large shopping malls, for instance. Both exhibit extremely violent tendencies. And, of course, both overeat.

When considered closely, though, it becomes clear that the biggest differences lie within these similarities. Humans tend to roam shopping malls in search of bargains or to kill time, while zombies roam shopping malls in search of humans to kill and eat. Humans become violent when their belief system is questioned, while zombies' violent tendencies arise from craving live human brains. And when humans overeat, it is usually due to an overabundance of buffet items, while a zombie's gluttony involves devouring as much still-moving human prey as possible.

These factors make human coexistence with zombies unlikely. Yet the human race has proven time and again that it has an uncanny ability to adapt and turn difficult situations to its advantage. So only time will tell.

Bringing Up Zombie

In the mid '60s, an elderly human couple found a zombie baby and raised it in secret on their farm. It was fed pig brains and taught human behavior. This zombie eventually became a hunter of the living dead and a hero to the many humans he saved.

Coexistence Scenarios

Noted zombiologists have put forth the following scenarios in which zombies and humans might one day coexist.

Zombie Reservations

Zombies could be penned on isolated reservations where they would be allowed to roam among their own kind.

Pros: A plot of land where zombies are penned and studied might be valuable in controlling them in the event of a global outbreak. In the past, observing captive zombies has helped researchers understand zombie behavior.

Cons: Hunters and thrill seekers might flock to such reservations to exploit the living dead for sport. Rambunctious, careless extreme-sports enthusiasts might spread the zombie virus outside the reservation.

Controlled State or Zombie Nation

In this scenario, zombies would be given their own state in which they would govern themselves while being heavily monitored by border patrol.

Pros: Prolonged socialization within their own kind away from humans might force zombies to feed upon one another, thus reducing the overall zombie population.

Cons: Because the zombie virus mutates so rapidly, allowing zombies to exist in close quarters with each other could result in a powerful, new zombie super-virus that could spread uncontrollably beyond the perimeter. Further, it is unlikely that taxpayers would support a statehood or sovereignty arrangement. Religious fundamentalists would likely object to allowing the soulless walking dead to govern and procreate, viewing such rights as affronts to God and nature.

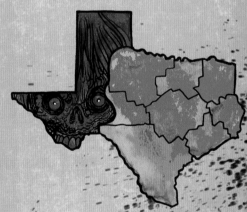

 The Controlled State solution would see portions of several states cordoned off for zombie habitation.

Future of Zombies—The Upside

Scientists believe that if they can stop zombies' urge to kill, zombie plagues may have practical applications. With the dwindling supply of fossil fuels, for instance, zombies might be used as an energy source to pull trains, buses and other forms of mass transportation.

Further, pacification of zombies could eliminate the need for humans to engage in undesirable or dangerous occupations such as crop picking or mining, freeing humans to enjoy leisure pursuits like bungee jumping, jet skiing and skydiving.

Carefully trained zombies could be used in space travel, setting up the infrastructure to colonize other planets without the need for bulky life-support apparatuses. And just imagine how alien life forms might be impressed by Earth creatures that can't be killed.

The medical applications zombies could provide are endless. If doctors could unlock the secret to reanimating dead flesh, they could produce organs that live forever inside the body, thus eliminating the need for moderation and healthy living.

Pictured here is the first zombie in space on a covert experimental mission. Could zombies like this represent the future of space exploration?

Zombie miners have already been tested by giant nickel corporations in Canada. This photo was snapped during one such secret test.

Robo-Zombies

Human scientists could conceivably augment undead flesh with mechanical prosthetics to create a new life form. They are currently working on such technology, hoping to perfect the ultimate combination of man and machine. Perfectly controlled and enhanced zombies could be used for everything from zombie crossing guards and frontline infantry troops to zombie daycare workers and busboys. The possibilities are endless. Information leaks suggest that some of these automatons are already being used in deep-sea exploration.

We must take care, however, not to let these flesh-fused machines take over and bring about the end of human existence. The only thing more dangerous than a zombie plague would be a robo-zombie plague.

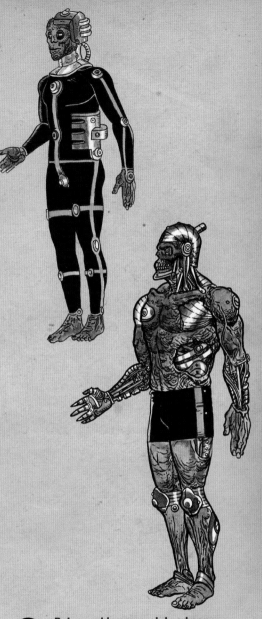

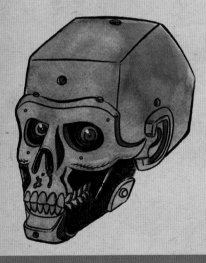

Robo-zombie remains have been found in and around battlefields as far back as the Vietnam War. This robo-zombie skull was unearthed in a rice paddy outside of Saigon. Neither the United States nor the Vietnamese government has claimed responsibility.

Robo-zombie research has been ongoing for decades. Pictured here is a robo-zombie manufactured in the 1970s and a model from the 1990s.

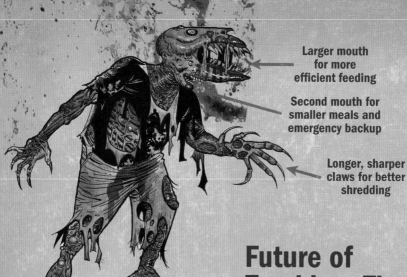

Larger mouth for more efficient feeding

Second mouth for smaller meals and emergency backup

Longer, sharper claws for better shredding

Rear toehold for scaling and climbing

Nano-bots' ability to manipulate a host to their own advantage could result in advanced zombies with extraordinary abilities.

Future of Zombies—The Downside

Like humans, zombies possess the ability to mutate into a stronger, fitter zombie species. They may evolve into quicker, stronger and smarter killing machines, making peaceful coexistence unlikely. They may even develop a resistance to head-smashing.

Natural zombie evolution could bring the onset of the apocalypse, especially if combined with advanced technological innovations such as nanotechnology. Microscopic robots, called "nano-bots," act as super-regenerative cells that can self-replicate to repair damaged tissue. Anything from a severed finger to massive head trauma can be repaired using nano-bots. There is even a theory that early nanotechnology experiments may have caused the first zombie outbreak.

Could Zombies Evolve Beyond Eating Human Flesh?

As zombies adapt and mutate, it is possible that their dietary habits could change too, perhaps even shifting to a humanless diet. We can only hope that zombie evolution takes this less sinister turn.

Evolved Super-Zombies

Scientists have experimented with fusing a nano-bot to a virus cell to create a nano-cyborg, which could outlive its host by about a month. Although the flesh was dead, nano-cellular activity remained. As this technology develops, it could result in a factory line of living dead. It could also create super-zombies that are highly adaptable and resistant to traditional forms of re-death. Such nano-fueled zombies would be unstoppable.

💀 Advanced adaptations for acquiring live flesh might lead to freakishly hideous zombies like this one, which can elongate its arm to catch prey.

💀 Nano-fueled zombies might also assimilate other life forms. This zombie absorbed at least one other zombie as well as a pigeon and a rat.

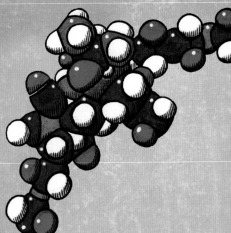

The currently known molecular structure of the zombie virus. Scientists are working hard to complete the map.

A Cure for Zombieism?

The zombie virus attacks live humans unpredictably, mutating so fast that scientists have been unable to completely map its molecular structure, so a medical cure for zombieism is unlikely in the near future. The only presently known "cure" is to blow off the heads of the infected.

By the time a living human has fully turned into a zombie, it is too late to simply return him or her to normal. Death has already claimed the victim's soul, and nature has begun the slow process of breaking down the body through decay. A "cure" might entail finding a way to eliminate zombies' need to ingest human flesh and brain matter. Then zombies could become vessels that humankind could exploit for its own purposes.

To this end, scientists have been working tirelessly on a zombie pharmaceutical drug that replicates the sensation of eating brains. A "brain patch" slowly releases the drug into the zombie's central nervous system, weaning it from human head goo.

The process is still in its earliest stages. If it is perfected, some day humans may see the pacification of zombies. We may even progress to a point where, for a government stipend, you could donate your afterlife as a controlled zombie in service to your country—not unlike organ donors today.

Could medical breakthroughs allow for the productive integration of zombies into human society?

This cryogenically frozen zombie, one of many, was given a "zombie death" virus being tested by a major drug company. The zombie was released from the facility and followed until it fell to the ground and froze. Could this be the genesis of a cure for zombieism? Only time will tell.

Repopulating the World

Before any major repopulation efforts can occur in the wake of a Zombie Apocalypse, surviving humans will have to make sure there are no zombies left anywhere on the planet. If even one brain-chomper exists, humanity remains at risk. But once the cleanup effort is undertaken, all available energy should be devoted to repopulating the world. Reproduction must be every human's top priority.

But who will deliver the babies? Doctors and hospital workers will be among the first victims of a zombie outbreak, having fallen victim to wave after wave of patients suffering from "flu-like" symptoms. Farmers, who make their homes on vast fields, are also unprotected. Lacking these and other skilled workers will make emerging from the wreckage of the zombie onslaught difficult.

But daunting as it may be, humans will rise to the challenge—as they have always done—to repopulate and rebuild the world anew. Someday in the far future we shall know a world in which our children do not live in daily fear of being devoured by zombies. But until that day has come, vigilance remains imperative.

After the zombies are defeated, a mass cleanup will be needed to rid the world of virus-ridden corpses. New forms of waste management and disposal will need to be implemented to avert future outbreaks. The cleanup will need to be done quickly to reduce the risk of further health and environmental problems stemming from the great numbers of rotting bodies littering the planet.

About the Authors

Rob Sacchetto is the accomplished, world-renowned illustrator famous for turning regular people into hideous zombies at www.zombieportraits.com. His army of the undead began in November 2006, and currently includes over 600 paintings that grace mantles and gross out guests all over the world. His work has been featured in Jonathan Maberry's *Zombie CSU* and the documentary *Zombiemania.* Rob is also a talented tattoo flash artist and is working on a new comic book entitled *Rob Sacchetto's Cape Fear.* He was born in Sudbury, Ontario, Canada, where he still lives with his wife and agent, Andrea.

Andrea Sacchetto represents artists and their work through her online agency www.wayoutthere.ca. She wrote as a freelance journalist for over ten years, and spent almost as many in advertising and promotion. She is the voice behind www.zombieportraits.com and spends most of her time promoting all things zombie.